T0147483

INVISIBLE MONEY

and How It Affects You

INVISIBLE MONEY

and How It Affects You

Robert A. Reilly

iUniverse, Inc.

New York   Bloomington

Invisible Money
And How It Affects You

iUniverse books may be ordered through booksellers or by contacting:

iUniverse
1663 Liberty Drive
Bloomington, IN 47403
www.iuniverse.com
1-800-Authors (1-800-288-4677)

ISBN: 978-1-4401-5289-4 (sc)
ISBN: 978-1-4401-5286-3 (ebook)

Printed in the United States of America

iUniverse rev. date: 6/19/2009

Table of Contents

Introduction

As children we read Ben Franklin's famous quote "a penny saved is a penny earned."

Ben's quote is one of the greatest statements ever made about money. So I decided to write a book based on his statement, giving it my own interpretation so to speak. To me Ben's profound quote is about "invisible" money.

Let's say you own a house free and clear, thereby eliminating a mortgage payment of $1,000 a month or $12,000 a year. That's money you don't need to earn. It would take a $300,000 certificate of deposit earning four percent annually to generate $12,000 a year in income before taxes. And no one can steal the $12,000 in "invisible money" with say the shenanigans of a sophisticated Ponzi scheme.

All it takes to get the "invisible" loot is self-discipline and keeping your wallet closed except for essentials and some affordable extras. The peace of mind a debt free life brings is worth a king's ransom.

It's not easy being tight with money in America. The government, which is often subservient to business and other special interest groups, really doesn't want us to be too thrifty although it won't admit it. After all too much thrift can harm the overall economy we're told. An estimated seventy percent of gross domestic product (goods and services) comprises consumer spending. That's why we don't see a "penny saved is a penny earned" slogan on billboards nation wide. That's why we don't hear members of Congress and the president make thrift a constant theme in their speeches. And that is why there is no coin or greenback with "God wasn't a spend thrift" etched on it.

If Washington and Wall Street cut out the graft and greed consumers wouldn't have to be counted on to spend so much money.

Just as working men and women can create "invisible" money so can the government. The same principle about "invisible" money that's applied to individuals can also be applied to the government. Government always talks about cutting spending while at the same time it increases spending to a level not seen in human history. It's more about politics than economics. The problem is convincing elected officials to change the way things are done. If Washington would change its ways "invisible" money would flow like water over the Hoover Dam.

The talk in Washington about reducing spending usually centers on reducing or eliminating Social Security payments and Medicare, two of the most successful government programs in history. Eliminating those programs would place the nation at a domestic security risk.

There are better ways to cut spending while at the same time position the country to provide what should be basic human rights—the right to a post secondary education, the right to necessary medical care, and the right to have a day in court without going bankrupt from legal fees.

The purpose of this book is to take the three professions that are the foundation of the country—post secondary education (including on-the-job training), health care and the law—and discuss ways in which they could be restructured to literally save billions of dollars thereby placing them on a more sound financial footing while reducing the national debt.

It's like killing two birds with one stone.

This book isn't about how individuals can create "invisible" money. It's about large institutions and the change in public policy needed to reduce the cost of higher education, medical services, and legal education.

Higher education is the next housing crisis. Millions of students are borrowing money to attend on campus classes that will place them in lifelong debt. This is occurring at a time when jobs are disappearing and technology is doing jobs that humans once performed.

Robert A. Reilly

The first chapter, "The Virtual University," lists ways the government could drastically reduce the cost of providing a higher education resulting in "invisible" money. If state and the federal governments want to they can bring the university into every home in America with world-class instruction 24/7. Never in the history of the world has so much education been made available for so little money. But you wouldn't know that by watching millions of college age students filling out loan forms that will place them in hock for most of their working lives. It's the campus lifestyle more than the education itself that students are after for the most part. This is a distinction that hasn't been made enough times. Education has been packaged and sold like a physical product you would buy at a store rather than the priceless intangible that it is.

The title of the second chapter, "Stay Away From the Whore House," discusses my real life training. Education involves more than taking classes, learning a skill or passing examinations. It's going places, meeting people, adapting to a new environment, coming to grips with achievement and disappointment. It was the best time of my life for learning. Real life experiences teaches a person about intangibles such as empathy, to respect other people who are different, to know that intelligence comes in many forms, and that there are limits to what individuals and nations can achieve. The greatest and most successful men and women in the world learned from real life experiences such as the great Chief Justice John Marshall, the great President Abe Lincoln to today's Oprah Winfrey, one of the most influential persons in the world, to Dolly Parton, a down home type of woman who built a $250 million business empire. Intelligence and experience will trump grades and a diploma nearly all the time. If the government adopted a public policy to encourage high school graduates to travel, meet people from all walks of life and work at public services jobs students would add to their university or other post secondary education. In a global society students need more than just a marketable skill.

I decided to write a brief autobiography in chapter two highlighting my school and on-the-job training experiences to explain in human, rather than in academic terms, the complexity and wide scope of an education.

Chapter 3 affects everyone. The world knows the health care industry is breaking our nation's financial back. In the old days people took their health into their own hands because they didn't have urgent care and large hospitals. Many people living in the 1700 and 1800s led long lives, often 80 plus years, under the most primitive and unhealthy conditions. That should tell us we often use medical services we don't need. "Modern Medicine: It Makes Me Sick," discusses some of the harm modern medicine can do to patients while at the same time suggest ways to make medical care more affordable.

Chapter 4 explains part of the reason hiring a lawyer is too expensive for most Americans. It all begins with the training of lawyers that has become so expensive that future lawyers can't accept lower paying public service jobs because they have tens of thousands of dollars in student loans to pay off. "A Rule That Is Ruining the Legal Profession" discusses how most of the individual states, with the help of the federal government, are unnecessarily jacking up the price of a legal education.

The cost of training a lawyer, for the most part, will remain high unless there is a change in public policy.

In summary, looking for "invisible" money should be a national priority. The federal government will even go into deeper debt by paying higher interest rates on the vast amount of money now being borrowed.

"Increased rates could translate into hundreds of billions of dollars more in government spending for countries like the United States, Britain and Germany," wrote the New York Times in a front- page article on June 4, 2009.

"Even a single percentage point increase could cost the Treasury an additional $50 billion annually over a few years—and, eventually, an additional $170 billion annually.

"This could put unprecedented pressure on other government spending, including social programs and military spending, while also sapping economic growth by forcing up rates on debt held by companies, homeowners and consumers."

High government officials are worried about the situations. The USA Today newspaper in its June 4, 2009 edition said: "Federal Reserve Chairman Ben Bernanke warned Congress that it must act promptly to narrow the federal budget deficit or risk losing the confidence of financial markets."

The paper quoted Bernanke as saying to the House Budget Committee: "In order to make lenders willing to continue to finance us at a reasonable rates, we do have to persuade them that we are serious about returning to a more balanced fiscal situation going forward. Unless we demonstrate a strong commitment to fiscal sustainability in the longer term, we will have neither financial stability nor healthy economic growth."

It seems that state and federal governments must be completely restructured to fill 21st century needs in order to get the balanced fiscal stability Bernanke says the nation needs. We should begin the restructuring with education, medicine and law.

I sincerely hope you find this book interesting. I would appreciate any comments you would like to make. My mailing address is Robert Reilly, P.O. Box 309, Phoenix, Arizona. 85001.

The editorial content and opinions expressed in this book are the sole responsibility of Robert Reilly.

(1)
The Virtual University

Imagine having a college tour like this that would generate billions of dollars in "invisible" money.

"Good morning ladies and gentleman. My name is Homer Jones. I am going to brief you this morning on the new University of the United States of America, or good old UUSA. We haven't got a mascot yet or a university song but we're working on it.

Twenty of you were invited to take this tour based on the letters you wrote to your congressional representatives complaining about the high cost of a college education. Unfortunately two people couldn't make it. One woman tragically committed suicide from being overwhelmed with $500,000 in debt. A middle- aged man suffered a stroke upon receiving a home foreclosure notice. Part of my job today is to tell you what we are doing in Washington to help relieve some money woes by virtually eliminating the cost of higher education.

 "Yes, the gentleman in the back. You have a question?"

 "You mean to say we can send our kids to college for nearly nothing? You must be kidding?"

 "I'm not kidding. Because of the great advances in technology we can, and will, offer as close as possible a free university education to every student who is a United States citizen regardless of where he or she lives, regardless of their age or physical handicap or formal education. All a student needs is desire, a willingness to learn and be a good citizen.

 "Now before I answer any questions I'm going to do something a little different. Instead of telling you what needs to be done to attend the university I'm going to tell you what doesn't have to be done.

 "Hold on to your hats. You will never have to write a check for tuition. Many thanks for the loud applause. And the young man in the back with red hair. I enjoyed your beautiful whistle. Just like a bird. Now you won't need to apply for student loans. You won't have to purchase textbooks. They will be digitalized and downloaded. You don't have to worry about grades or standardized test scores. Everyone is admitted who applies provided they pass a routine background check. There is no application fee. There will be a small administration fee we estimate at $300 a year for such things as a computer hook-up and earphones. Financial assistance is available for anyone who cannot afford the administration fee. Any questions. Yes, the lady in the second row."

"When can I sign up?"

 "Four-times a year, beginning with the second quarter of this coming year. Now please follow me into the room that is the heart and soul of the UUSA. A nice short walk wasn't it? We have 10 full time staff members and about 20 part-time helpers that we use when necessary. To your right are some of the 3,000 courses we will be offering on line, including those in medicine, nursing, law and engineering. I have in my hand seven discs of a course of 84 lectures on quantum mechanics. Workbooks, study guides and sample tests are provided. Students can log on to the computer and get an up to a minute rundown on how they are faring in each course. Are they behind, ahead or right where they need to be? The lectures are available 24/7 on computer and can be run once or 1,000 times. We will have live lectures over the Internet. Students who sign up for a class will be placed in contact with other students in the class. They can text message or e-mail each other and, if they live in the same area, meet face-to-face. We have tutors for the courses. Robots called Hedy, named after the 1940s and 1950s Hollywood actress Hedy Lamarr, one of the most beautiful women in the world at the time. The reason we singled out Ms. Lamarr was because she was also brilliant in math and co-developed a device making it harder to detect radio-guided torpedoes. If she were alive today, we would love to have Ms. Lamarr as either a math instructor or as a student of quantum mechanics.

"Look behind you and you will see a telephone. Pick it up and press number one and you will hear Hedy answer a question from a student. Wait for a few seconds and you will hear the student ask another question and Hedy will respond again. If she doesn't know the answer, which is rare, she says she will get back with the student within 24 hours.

"Incredible," said an elderly gentleman. "I never believed I'd see something like this in my lifetime."

Mr. Jones continued his remarks. "The motto of UUSA is 'what you know and can do is what counts, not how you learned it.' We place competence over grades, tests scores and credentials. If you know a foreign language you can take a spoken or written test and get credit. If you are a paralegal and know contract law or legal research you can take a test and earn credits toward a law degree. If you happen to be a Bill Gates or a Steve Jobs you can put together a portfolio and we will award a PhD degree. If you are a Dolly Parton and succeeded in business, you would be awarded a business degree. These aren't honorary degrees my friends. These are the same degrees with the same weight as a person who took classes and graduated. Most of what people learn in life was learned outside the classroom. Just because something was learned in a classroom doesn't make it more legitimate than other types of learning. Millions of people outside of academia are equal or better instructors than those inside academia. Just ask students who learned how to work on sophisticated aircraft and nuclear submarines while serving in the military.

"I like to make some parting comments. The world has changed. Universities must change also. They are basically obsolete. We now have virtual universities that can reproduce classrooms and administrative offices on your computer. Learning knows no limits. We can pipe in live lectures from an Oxford professor or an ordinary citizen who just achieved something extra ordinary. We value knowledge and experience over academic credentials. We can, and will, reduce the cost of a college education by more than 90 percent for people who are seeking the most for their educational dollar. It's either that or bankrupt generations of students and force state legislatures to needlessly spend money they don't have. Will this be the end of a campus education? No. An estimated 10 to 15 percent of students currently on campus today actually need to be there. The vast majority of students don't need to be there, thousands wouldn't be there if it wasn't for parent pressure. Yet if a student wishes to pay $2,800 for a course of study that can be had for virtually nothing, we say go right ahead and buy it. This is America. But they won't be eligible for a government backed student loan or grant. We're broke as a nation. Fifty percent of families can't survive financially for a month if they lost their income. About 10 million people have payday loans. Twenty eight million people don't have a bank account. Forty eight million Americans don't have health insurance. The federal government is borrowing or printing trillions of dollars because it's flat broke. We need to restructure our institutions and we are going to begin with higher education. Anyone who wants a college education can get one. Every state will be required to have a virtual university or face severe cuts in federal financial support.

"Nike's phrase 'just do it' is also our motto, thanks to the sneaker company who gave us their blessing. A tape of this meeting will be sent to groups nationwide. We're sending out 20 million e-mails outlining the program and the president of the United States will be delivering a speech on all the major networks two weeks from Tuesday at 9 p.m. eastern time. His theme is "a college education for everyone who wants it.' Good day and good luck."

Is the above college tour far fetched? No. Everything mentioned during the tour is possible and much of it is already taking place. In California there are virtual law schools that reach students throughout the world.

Will the government step in and force a major change in higher education? It's unlikely anything will be done on the federal level in the near future. The education lobby is so strong and Americans have been bamboozled for so long about higher education it will be hard to get out the facts of life necessary to bring about wide spread change. However, when new technology faces off against the status quo, new technology eventually wins out over the long haul. And eventually it will in this case. America can no longer afford to do things like it did in the past.

Major advances in higher education already occurred with one of the biggest bombshells hitting on April 4, 2001 that was heard around the world. The Massachusetts Institute of Technology (MIT), one of the most elite and expensive universities in the United States, announced a decision it would make all 1,600 of its classes free on the Internet. The program was billed "MIT Open Course Ware (MITOCW).

"As president of MIT, I have come to expect top-level innovative and intellectually entrepreneurial ideas from the MIT community," said Charles Vest, in a press release. "When we established the Counsel on Educational Technology at MIT, we charged a sub-group with coming up with a project that reached beyond our campus classrooms.

"Open Course Ware is not exactly what I had expected," he continued. "It is not what many people may have expected. But it is typical of our faculty to come up with something as bold and innovative as this, Open Course Ware looks counter-intuitive in a market driven world. It goes against the grain of current material values. But it is really consistent with what I believe is the best about MIT. It is innovative. It expresses our belief in a way education can be advanced—by constantly widening access to information and by inspiring others to participate. Simply put, Open Course Ware is a natural marriage of American higher education and the capabilities of the World Wide Web."

MIT courses are available to anyone but no credit is awarded and no degree is granted. A regular four- year course of study would be worth about $150,000 in saved tuition. The education itself: "priceless."

I've paid attention to higher educational for more than 30 years and the most remarkable achievement I encountered was in the early 1990s when I wrote a feature story about Joyce Swann and her family. I looked up Mrs. Swann on the Internet a few weeks ago. I found this article in "Home School World," a publication for home schooled kids and their parents.

"The Swann children typically receive high school diplomas at age eleven, bachelor's degrees at age fifteen, and master's degrees at age sixteen. The vast majority of academic work had been completed at home."

In a column in "Home School World" Mrs. Swann wrote in 1993. "A few weeks ago an acquaintance asked my husband how much it was going to cost us for our ten children to earn their bachelor's and master's degrees. After some quick mental calculations, John responded that the total cost would be about $100,000—in other words, $10,000 per child, or less than $2,000 per year of college education."

Mrs. Swann is another example of an ordinary citizen who has a certain genius, a genius that could benefit the nation and a genius that should have been presented to the nation. She taught her children while they sat at the family's dining room table. I talked with people who knew the family. They said the Swann children successfully competed academically with students 30 and 40 years of age.

The Swann family achieved a remarkable feat with basically correspondence courses. Can you imagine what the family would have achieved with the advantage of a virtual university? They would have had regular face-to-face meetings with their professors, fellow students and administrators. A sort of educational cherry on top.

Here is another higher education program you may not know about. New York State for years has had an innovative approach with its New York Regents External Degree Program, a national examining program. Students can earn college credit and degrees by passing examinations. There are also other ways to earn college credit in such fields as nursing, electronics engineering, technology and nuclear engineering technology plus traditional courses in business and the arts and sciences. A portfolio assessment allows students to earn credit for practical experience.

The New York State Regents External Degree Program would be even stronger if incorporated into a virtual campus.

Some educators, such as Dr. Vest, believe the best way to earn a college degree is to attend classes on campus rather than off campus.

"Let me be clear," said Dr. Vest of the Open Course Ware Program. "We're not providing an MIT education on the web. We are providing our core material that are the infrastructure that under grids an MIT education. Real education requires interaction, the interaction that is a part of American teaching. We think that Open Course Ware will make it possible for faculty here and elsewhere to concentrate even more on the actual process of teaching, on the interactions between faculty and students that are the real core of learning."

There is no question Dr. Vest makes a good argument for on campus instruction. But a good argument is not a universal truth. The collaboration Dr. Vest talks about isn't the same type of collaboration needed for a history or political science course. And not all scientists need to be on campus.

Thomas Edison, an authentic genius, being one such person. Edison, who had about 1,100 patents and was one of the most influential persons in human history, wasn't that high on learning inside a school of any kind. He was kicked out of school three months after he started and was home schooled by his mother, a former teacher, according to Edison's biography. Instead of going to college he built his own laboratory in Menlo Park, New Jersey where he developed the electric light system and invented the first phonograph. He didn't need a lot of professors and students around him to succeed. Edison thought the best way to learn was by observing nature and working with his hands. It would be interesting to know how Edison would have viewed the virtual campus as a learning tool?

For most people it would be more advantageous to become an independent learner off campus. Most students leave college for good after graduating. They must figure things out for themselves for the rest of their lives without the help and guidance of professors. The earlier they can develop independent learning skills the better chance for success later in life.

Of course on campus courses are good for some people. At MIT and other scientific institutions students and professors work together on cutting edge projects such as nanotechnology and bioinformatics that are beyond the academic reach of the vast majority of people who attend a university. In the rarefied scientific world it's easy to understand the advantages of a close collaboration among professors and students.

Downsizing the nation's universities and replacing them with virtual campuses won't be easy economically or politically. The major universities in this country are huge. There are hundreds of billions of dollars in plant and equipment. It is mind-boggling and scary to think the physical structure of nearly 3,500 institutions of higher education in this country are in many ways obsolete and too expensive to maintain. Virtual campuses don't need physical repairs, utilities, and large maintenance staffs. Students don't have to travel to get there. And most academic course material can be placed on a computer.

And colleges are labor intensive with thousands of professors teaching small numbers of students at a time. A single professor at a virtual university could potentially reach millions of students at one time. The $100,000 a year professor plus benefits may soon become rare on campus.

Large libraries and their staffs also aren't needed. It won't be long before every book ever written will be available to download into the computer from Internet sites such and Amazon and Google.

It's hard to admit when your time is up. But the time of the university as we know it has passed on like the dinosaur. Only a small number of campuses are needed in their present form.

The big question is what to do with the people who would lose their jobs. Skills would need to be transferred to other professions and the government would need to provide a list of projects such as rebuilding the inner cities, tutoring youngsters, tending to the elderly and creating research facilities outside academia. Corporations could be encouraged to develop their own universities and employ professors to instruct their workers. Corporations both large and small should train their own workers like employers did through apprenticeship programs in the old days.

Will it be the cost of keeping the colleges in their present form that gives us the final push off the financial cliff? It's possible. Students must borrow tens of thousands of dollars to earn a degree for a shot at a middle class life although the chances of them obtaining a high- paying job to pay off the loan is diminishing by the day. Entry into the middle class should be based on merit not by how much a student is willing to borrow money. But few people look at it that way. Colleges and universities hold a special place in the hearts of Americans. It's almost like a religion. The educational lobby is powerful. Government officials in Washington don't even want to talk about alternative education. It's among the hottest of the hot potato issues. The idea of higher education is to get enough fannies into the seats.

But strong lobbying groups and timid officials at the state and federal levels, I believe, will eventually be forced to succumb to the forces of nature. The virtual university is here and it won't go away. The more governments resist recognizing the reality of the virtual university, the more painful the punishment will be for being so short sighted. But as we have seen time and time again America will risk its financial future to do what it wants justified or not. We got into the current financial mess by being reckless with money rather than prudent and there is no indication things are about to change anytime soon.

(2)
Stay Away From The Whore House

For me school was a bad fit from the beginning.

I learned in first grade I was never going to be one of the brightest students. My mother told my teacher I should repeat the first grade. A few years later when we moved to upstate New York she wanted me held back again but the principal of the school said: "let's first see how he does in fourth grade." In his eyes I may have been too big to fit in a third grade chair.

Although very few people knew it at the time I was good at reading and could grasp information quickly. Most of what I was given to read bored me. My interests lay elsewhere, mainly with major league baseball but

I instinctively knew reading comprehension would ultimately be my salvation

That didn't matter to my mom. To her I was a slow learner and if it took me twenty years to get through twelve grades so be it.

Today in an era of social promotion of students and just about every kid is considered a winner regardless of his or her ability, my mom would be considered cruel for damaging my-self esteem. My mom called them as she saw them and wasn't a sympathetic person when it came to practical issues like doing well in school. My mother, who spoke and read Swedish as well as she did English, walked four miles to school in all kinds of weather, used an outhouse and tended to farm animals under primitive conditions. You couldn't have your head stuck in the clouds and survive on an Iowa farm in those days.

My mom wasn't the only the person to believe the bulb in my brain hadn't been turned on. Some of her friends slipped me a little money to get lost not wanting to talk to a little kid that didn't know much. I took some abuse for my poor grades from fellow classmates. In those days the smart kids had advanced learning materials while us dumb kids were given easier material to work with although we were officially in the same grade.

Years later when I looked back on those years there was some justification for the attitude toward me. My two older sisters, Ruth and Mary, and my older brother John, performed much better in school and had vastly superior social skills. So without much talent on the social front and apparently without much gray matter upstairs it's not surprising there weren't many people inviting me over to their house to light up the room.

I spent my days throwing a rubber ball against the side of the house, learned something about every player on the Brooklyn Dodger baseball team, played board games, joined the basketball and baseball teams at school and dreamed of being Willie Mays or Frank Sinatra. I don't remember reading a book from cover to cover the whole time I was in elementary or high school. I did, however, read some history far beyond my grade level. My overall reading skills kept improving that helped later on.

Following my sophomore year in high school we moved to Vero Beach, Florida because of my father's poor health.

I had to quickly adapt to the adult world. I financially supported my mother and father for a few months. My mom was a stay at home type. Kids helping support the family wasn't unusual in those days. Lots of kids were in the same boat. I got a night job during the week waiting tables at Duffy's Restaurant where some of the Dodgers ate during spring training. Manager Walter Alston came in a couple of times and ate alone. Most of the Dodgers who ate there were rookies or players on the minor league roster.

Most of my salary at the restaurant was actually paid for by the waitresses who gave me a percentage of their tips for cleaning off the tables and keeping the water glasses filled. Some of the waitress needed the money more than I did. They were young, married with children and wore white dresses. By the end of the night they had aching feet and would sit down around a table together in the rear of the restaurant and talk. There was a mom in her late teens who was having a tough go of it with an abusive husband. On the way out the door I would slip her a dollar or two once in a while. She never said thank you but there were tears in her eyes. The waitresses weren't shy talking about their disappointment s in life. There was trouble with kids. There was trouble with elderly parents and there was trouble with bill collectors. It was like a front row seat at a soap opera. The restaurant owner was a skinny guy who put on an apron when the cook didn't show up. If you're kind of lazy you don't want to own a restaurant. That's hard money.

A friend of mine from New York, Butch Berry, had moved to Vero Beach with his mother. He had the greatest job in the world; spring training batboy for the Dodgers. His mother somehow knew Buzzie Bavasi, an executive with the team who lived to age 93. I'd go out to Holman Stadium with Butch and walk among the players. The one who stood out the most was pitcher Don Drysdale, a tall, good-looking guy who drew a lot of fans around him. Fans can be nice but they can also be nasty, particularly if they are ignored when trying to get an autograph. It's the first time I witnessed the downside of celebrity. One night Butch took me inside the old barracks where the players stayed and Walter O'Malley, owner of the team, came up to me and said "kid, you need to lose some weight." I weighed about 85 pounds at the time. Butch later collapsed and died while standing in line at a military academy. His mother, who owned show horses, also died at a young age. They had money but their lives were cut short. Death doesn't discriminate.

On weekends I worked at the Piggly Wiggly Supermarket packing grocery bags. The manager stood behind a glass cage on an elevated platform where he could see just about everything going on in the store. He never said much to me but gave me about the best advice I'd ever received. He said "pay your bills on time and don't throw your money around on bad things." (That's advice is more important today since the computer can scan credit card charges and determine if the card holder is living a risky life by spending money at the gambling casino or strip joint. A risky lifestyle may trump paying bills on time when it comes to getting credit).

I taught myself to stretch a dollar, shop, pay bills and buy a car, a beat up Oldsmobile with weak breaks. We lived in the sticks with snakes for neighbors. My uncle also lived in Vero Beach but he was a rather distant and sickly figure who had his own problems. I grew to like Vero Beach. I had joined the summer Babe Ruth League and was selected by a team sponsored by First Federal Savings. Then my mom and dad decided to go back east and my life really changed.

It's one thing to work at supermarket with kids you horse around with at school. It's another thing to suddenly be side by side with some of the sharpest people on the planet. We moved to Washington D.C. where I would get to meet some of the most influential people in the country.

The experience didn't set me on a path to riches. It didn't lead me up a career ladder. What it did was help me gain confidence, question authority, go against conventional wisdom, and make tough and realistic decisions without worrying about what people thought.

I picked a lot of brains in my youth. It wasn't book learning that kept me out of the messes. It was life experience and some luck, to know when the sun was shinning and when the dark clouds were about to roll in. You get the hang of it by learning from other people's experiences and poor choices. I realized at a young age I was probably going to be living life close to the edge like a man walking a tightrope. I saw rich people lose their money. I saw injuries ending promising athletic careers. That getting to the top is one thing but staying there is another. And there was always a price to pay for anything of value.

I thought the summer of 1957 was going to be a disaster. Washington was hot and humid in the summer. I didn't know anyone my own age. It would be tough adjusting to a new school in the senior year. I had so little time to fit in. My sisters and brother were already settled in. John was in the Army and stationed at Ft. McNare in military intelligence. Ruth and Mary worked for the federal government.

A few days after I arrived my brother hosted a party for some of his friends. Ted Venetoulis, who later was elected Baltimore County Executive and ended up being a legend in Maryland politics, said an executive at CBS needed a fill-in copyboy for the summer. My brother said I needed a job. Mr. Venetoulis then introduced me to a secretary at CBS' Washington bureau who attended the party. She arranged an interview for me. Three days I met Theodore Koop, an executive at the network and the fellow responsible for developing the news show "Face the Nation." The interview lasted about ten minutes. I filled out a short employment form and immediately became an employee at what was then considered the gold standard of network television news. I had been in Washington less than a week.

Today I probably would not have gotten within five floors of a top CBS executive. Back then the copyboy was located in the middle of things. A small office used by European correspondent Eric Sevareid when he was in town was about six feet to the right of me. To the left was the office of "Face the Nation" producer Ted Ayers. He and Mr. Koop had scored one of the biggest journalistic coups of the decade at the end of May and the staff was still talking about it when I arrived. Correspondent Bob Schieffer described the coup in his book "Face the Nation."

"Koop called me in one day in early May 1957 with a pleasant surprise. He told me that he and Ayers had a commitment from the Russian Embassy that the Soviet Chairman, Nikita Khrushchev, would be available for a free and unrehearsed film interview in the Kremlin in late May. We would have to send a crew to Moscow to produce the program. The Soviet government would produce the film crew, but the production would be managed by CBS. The chairman would answer questions with no strings attached."

Newspapers across the country wrote about the interview that Schieffer called "a smashing success." The story was controversial. Schieffer said the top brass at CBS feared if enough political pressure from the far right was applied the federal government could strip the company of its broadcast license. I hate to admit it but I don't recall the controversy and I never met Schieffer.

But for the first time in my life I was in daily contact with serious and talented people who were well versed in national and international affairs. It was an adult world of the highest order. It was a life changing experience to say the least.

People would walk in and out of the wire room where I was working all day long to read stories from Teletype machines. My main job was to keep paper in the machines. Eventually I made some small editorial judgments by tearing a story from several printed at the same time and handed it to the news desk. Other times an editor would ask me to keep track of a developing story and provide him with relevant updates.

One of the fun parts of the job was hearing bits and pieces about some of the network's famed journalists such as Edward R. Murrow, Sevareid, William L. Shirer and Bill Downs. The information I got was in tiny bits. "Murrow scored big in Vienna during the war." Then I'd later learn about his famous quote broadcast live in the United States and Canada from the scene of the action: "It's now 2:30 in the morning and Herr Hitler has not yet arrived." Or Murrow took some heat when he reported from a prisoner of war camp. "Rows of bodies stacked up like cord wood."

I never saw Murrow but I and thirteen other journalism fellows met his widow in 1979 at the Edward R. Murrow Center of Public Diplomacy at the Fletcher School of Law and Diplomacy, Tuffs University. We sat at a large table she used as a shield during the German bombing raids on London. She told us of the joys and difficulty being married to a world famous journalist and Murrow's rocky relationship with William S. Paley, the head of CBS.

Little did I know when I was fetching coffee and running errands at CBS that one day I'd be looking at some of Murrow's personal papers at the Fletcher School. Before I left my brief stint at the network its famed journalists had become bigger than life figures to me. Shirer and Sevareid filing live radio reports during the fall of France with Downs assigned to the paratroopers. Murrow had been in England describing the bombs dropping on London in a voice millions of people would never forget as long as they lived.

These were men who risked their lives and thought independently without regard for money. I could never be like them but I could try to be intellectually courageous like them in my own way and on my own level.

One afternoon when he was visiting Washington Mr. Sevareid motion to me to come over and sit. He asked me a few questions about myself and we discussed some baseball. I didn't ask him any questions. I was smarter than that. Two words described Mr. Sevaeid. Reserved and dignified. He was a first rate intellectual and if I were teaching journalism today (I did so part-time for three years at Temple University) I would show some clips of his thoughtful analysis of world events and compare those to the hot air emitting from television pundits today.

Mr. Koop also asked me to sit down for a few minutes. He wanted to know if I had thought about going to college and then said he had graduated from the University of Iowa and it had a good journalism school.

I remembered vividly what he said. I earned a masters degree in journalism slightly less than eleven years later from the University of Iowa. I saw Mr. Koop for the last time at a social function in Iowa City. I asked him what had happened to his secretary Mary Beth to whom I owed a great deal of gratitude. He said she graduated from the Georgetown University's School of Foreign Service and had been posted at the U.S. Embassy in London.

In those days I loved popular music particularly Frank Sinatra and Perry Como. Country music, forget it. While I was at CBS there was a singer named Jimmy Dean who had a live Saturday night show from the network's Broadcast House on Brandywine Ave. where I was working. A staff member, I don't remember who, asked me if I wanted to make some extra money being a prop guy during the show. Naturally I said yes.

My first assignment was to climb up a catwalk and help pull a swing back and forth for one of the singers on the show. It was pretty easy money. I don't remember how much money I made a week between the CBS job and occasionally filling in on the Dean Show but it was pretty good for a 17-year-old kid with no talent. I do remember being paid $10 in lunch money each Saturday I worked.

I only talked to Dean a few times. While becoming familiar at a distance with him and his show I learned to appreciate the music of singer of Patsy Cline, a close friend of Dean's who later died at age 30 in a plane crash.

It's ironic that Dean, who was once a major force in country and western music, and Joe DiMaggio, one of the greatest baseball players who ever lived, will be remembered best by a generation of children as the "Sausage Man" and "Mr. Coffee."

Dean's food company eventually evolved into Consolidated Foods that renamed it the Sarah Lee Corporation.

I left CBS as quickly as I arrived and enrolled in high school for my senior year. A few weeks later CBS called and said there was a job opening and invited me back. My mother answered the call and said I had to graduate from high school. She didn't inform me of the call for several days knowing I would have quit high school in a heart -beat to return to CBS for whatever job was available.

I settled for a job as a part time soda jerk at a pharmacy near the apartment building where we lived. I learned to make milk shakes and ice cream sodas pretty easily. It was a fun job because there was a nightclub in the small shopping area and some of the entertainers would drop in and kid around. The women seemed a little loose and a lot of fun for an 18- year-old because they would say things I never heard a woman say before. Then late one afternoon a lieutenant in the Army Ranger Corp., built like a football linebacker, came storming in and demanded that I come outside into the parking lot where he was going to tear me apart. I'd had never seen the lieutenant before and had no idea what he was talking about. He kept screaming for three to four minutes until the store manager came over and convinced him to walk a few steps to the front of the cash register. After a few minutes, which seemed like an hour, the manager slowly escorted the lieutenant out the door. The manager never said a word to me about the incident. I wonder to this day what would have happened to me if the manager hadn't been there. I assume I'd have been a victim of mistaken identity. It was a good lesson on how life "can turn on a dime."

I attended classes at Anacostia Senior High School that eventually became one of the most crime- ridden areas in Washington. The area was starting to change demographically when I was there but there were still a number of middle class kids from military families that comprised the student body. I sat next to a girl who was accepted at Radcliff and in front of a short, over weight kid who was enrolled in a couple of science courses at George Washington University. One lad was accepted into the Air Force Academy.

In those days new students had to take a test. I was placed in two advanced classes, a classic D student mixed in with college bound youngsters. I was out of my league and played academic catch up all year. Good test scores don't always translate into good grades.

We had a homeroom teacher who had a face like the witch in the Wizard of Oz. I don't remember ever seeing her smile. She looked to be in her late 50s. But somehow she learned little things about all of us. One day I mentioned to one of my classmates my brother was thinking about going into business when he got out of the Army and had friends that were thinking the same thing. A week later my homeroom teacher started placing a copy of The Wall Street Journal on the corner of my desk in the morning without saying a word. I had never read The Journal before and started reading it. As time went on the articles became easier for me to understand. A wonderful character trait was hidden beneath that teacher's hard exterior. Unfortunately, we don't always discover such treasures in what appears to be unimpressive people who cross our paths.

Toward the end of the school year kids were getting ready for the senior prom. I didn't know any girls well enough to ask them out on such an important date. However this one girl asked me to take her to the prom. I was kind of naïve then and said yes. Well, a week before the big event she cancelled our date because she had been asked to the prom by the guy she had wanted to go with all along.

It was a good lesson in the dating game.

In case you haven't notice I leave a lot of names out. It's because I've forgotten them. The faces and events are clear. It's the names that have been lost. But it's funny how the mind works. Years ago I watched Tulane University play Trinity University in a tennis match. Trinity had a top- notch player. It took me an hour to recall the name of Chuck McKinley who was an All America in 1963. I remembered Chuck's name from one incident but I can't remember the names of most of the students in my senior class.

I decided to join the Army after graduating in the lower 25 percent of my class. But my enlistment was temporarily placed on hold.

Robert A. Reilly

A fellow senior and a total stranger came up to me and suggested I try to set up an interview with Connie B. Gay, a well known figure in country and western music, to see if I could get a job at one of his radio stations. The young lady had heard me make the morning announcements over the school public address system. Crazy as it seems I decided to give it a shot. I got the interview with Mr. Gay at his small office in Arlington, Virginia. After we talked for a bit he told me to go home and write him an essay on why I wanted to work at his country and western radio station WTCR in Huntington, West Virginia with studios in Ashland, Kentucky.

I wrote the letter with the help of my new mysterious friend and got the summer announcer's job. WTCR was a 5,000- watt station that had longer broadcast hours during the summertime therefore the need for an extra hand. The pay was $75 a week. Mr. Gay, I learned, was the manager for Jimmy Dean, Ms. Cline and Roy Clark of the eventual television show Hee Haw.

The day following my high school graduation Mr. Gay's son picked me up at my apartment and drove the dangerous roads to Ashland.

The trip to Asland wasn't pleasant. Gay's son and I didn't hit it off. In the old days I would have kept quiet with a stranger and let him talk. But for some reason, I wasn't so passive. I became a bit cantankerous. At the end of the long trip he hit me between the eyes with a solid zinger: "Everyone in the world knows what you know," he said and slammed the car door.

In less than a week I was on the air spinning records and making small talk to the audience between each song. All announcers had to read the short advertisements and keep a log as to the time the ad was read on air. One of my favorite advertisers was O.T. Kitchen's Used Car Lot. The owner had a sense of humor so we could be creative reciting the copy. Some advertisers liked a little humor saying it made them appear more human, more like a family member. The star of the station was Jimmy Oakes, a poor man's Arthur Godfrey who wore cowboy boots and a cowboy hat. He was folksy, the audience loved him and he sold a ton of advertisements when he wasn't on the air. He did a good job showing me the ropes that included shutting the transmitter off at the end of the broadcast day. He was nice to me but I thought he was a little miffed because I hadn't paid enough dues to be working at a 5,000-watt radio station right out of high school.

On Sundays the local reverends gave their weekly on air sermon. I committed a major sin on my first day with the reverends. I had correctly pronounced the name of the first on air reverend but mauled the name of his church calling it asspoltolic instead of apostolic. Needless to say I wasn't given a saintly look. For the next 24 hours I waited for some angry parishioners to phone to complain I had shown disrespect by mispronouncing the name of their church but it turned out the good people of Kentucky showed kindness toward a kid from the north who was green as the blue grass in the broadcast business.

Within three weeks I started selling some advertisements on a very limited basis to small businesses. The routine was to interview the owner or an employee of the firm to find out how the basic business operated. Then the idea was to locate an advertising angle personalizing the product to someone closely connected to the firm. Say a young couple sold pots and pans. Grandma was coming to visit her two grandchildren. Well, the advertising salesman in me would suggest having the announcer say grandma would only cook her favorite stew in the pot on sale at Charley's and use only the pan that goes with it for baking homemade bread.

It was enjoyable talking with small business owners, some of whom had taken the art of "stretching a dollar" to a new level. They were hard working, down to earth, and had creative ways to keep their business afloat. The Kentucky and Tennessee campus rivalry in sports consumed the interest of both states. Kentuckians and tough times weren't strangers. It was a good place to see where some of the strongest backbones in America were made. And after playing the records and hearing the songs of Johnny Cash, Patsy Cline and Tennessee Ernie Ford, sprinkled with antidotes courtesy of many of the people I had met, I could honestly say I had become "country when country wasn't cool."

I had rented an apartment. It was the first time I had been completely on my own. I had purchased a car that slowed down going up hills. My sister Ruth made the white- knuckle drive from D.C. to Ashland and I cooked her breakfast, the first time I had done that.

The Army lay ahead.

When I was young my older brother John had a big influence on me. He was bright, very articulate and had a lot of interesting friends who had great jobs such as working on Capitol Hill and at the White House. He wasn't in to college except for a good time and dropped out of Ryder University in Trenton, New Jersey. He went into the Army and graduated number one in his class in military intelligence, topping some students who had graduated from Ivy League schools, and had his pick of assignments. He chose Washington. And there was another bonus. Uncle Sam allowed him to wear civilian cloths and drive a civilian looking car on the job.

Many of John's friends lucked out like he did in the military. One of his best friends at Ryder, Russ Palermo, became a Naval officer in Washington. Rank didn't mean much after duty hours. It was like mud wrestling at its best. It was hard to tell what anyone wore after five o'clock. What mattered was if you could hold your own in a debate and had the stuff to survive among the brightest, most ambitious young men and women in the country. Washington was, and still is, a magnet for those with big ambitions and arrogance. Washington was big enough in those days to be interesting and small enough to make a lot of contacts and my brother and his friends did just that.

My goal was to go into military intelligence like my brother and his friends. It wasn't to be. The army captain who was scheduled to interview me for entry into a military intelligence program was called away on another assignment and I was shipped out to take a military physical examination in Baltimore that included the order spread your cheeks, referring to the ones below the waist. I was then assigned to Ft. Jackson, South Carolina, for basic training and then to Augusta, Georgia, where I worked as a supply clerk for a civilian lady by the name of Mrs. Ogletree. While at Ft. Gordon I became life long friends with bank executive Edwin Renn and his wife Rowena. She gave private singing lessons and it was there it finally dawned on me I wasn't going to be another Sinatra. But Ed and Rowena took me in as part of their family. I did quite a bit of babysitting for their three children and Ed talked quite a bit about his job. Eventually the Renns moved to Atlanta where he became a senior vice president in personal banking with one of his clients being baseball legend Hank Aaron and she gained prominence as a singer and choral director. It was another wonderful learning experience, one I couldn't have received in a classroom.

Less than a year later the Army transferred me to Korea as a morning report clerk at the headquarters of the First Calvary Division, the only outfit in the Army at the time facing "an armed and ready aggressor."

Before leaving for over seas I was immunized against numerous diseases. One of the physicians at the military dispensary said: "stay away from the whore houses. Venereal diseases are rampant in Korea" and added there were no vaccines yet available to cure some of the diseases. He explained in detail some of the consequences of being in the wrong place at the wrong time and with the wrong people. He provided details of soldiers being robbed by prostitutes, arrested in military police sweeps of bars, taken into custody for stealing government property and caught for possessing illegal drugs. His graphic warning against risky behavior stuck with me from then on.

I flew to San Francisco on the first leg of the trip to Korea. Usually soldiers of my low rank had to make the trip to Korea by boat, a terrible two-week experience for anyone subject to seasickness. As soon as I checked in I asked to see the soldier in charge of arranging passage. He was a slow talking tall fellow. I said to him right off the bat that if he could get me off the boat roster and on to an airplane flight I'd give him $10 and handed him a slip of paper with my name, rank and serial number on it. He didn't say anything but placed the slip of paper inside his pocket. Around midnight he came to my bunk and said "I got you on a flight now where is my $10." It was the best $10 I'd ever spent.

The flight was great. My assignment was to assist an officer's wife with two young children. That was easy. I made faces, played hide the stuffed animal game and told stories about two children who were on a magical ride to Toyko to see their dad so they could do wonderful things together.

We stopped in Hawaii and I thought about going absent without leave (AWOL) in Paradise, intoxicated by the tropical breezes. We landed briefly at Wake Island, a dot in the Pacific Ocean where American forces surrendered to the Japanese on December 23, 1941. There wasn't much on the island but a few old buildings and then we headed on to Tokyo for a four- day lay over. Some soldiers lucked out and got re-assigned from Korea to Tokyo, one of the plumb places to be fifteen years following Japan's surrender in World War 11. I tried but couldn't get reassigned and landed in Korea, a place that was still war torn six years after a shaky truce was signed that ended the shooting involving the two Koreas and United Nations forces headed by the U.S.

The environment was such a shock; muddy roads and a depressing Quonset hut where we lived, a lightweight prefabricated structure hot as hell in the summer and cold as ice in the winter. We had to climb a steep hill to go to the bathroom in all kinds of weather but at least the toilet was in doors.

Shortly after I had arrived at the First Calvary I was riding a bus to a Recreation Center to play some pool and asked a military recruiter heading in the same direction what was the best job available for an enlisted man on the post. He said military correspondent and a sports writer position was currently available at the Cavalier, the weekly newspaper serving the First Calvary division.

I had never written a news or feature story in my life but I thought I'd interview for the job. I was getting my morning reports in about noon (I was no Radar) so I knew it wouldn't be long before I'd be reassigned, likely to a combat outfit.

The fellow doing the interviewing for the newspaper job was Lt. Leon Howell, from Copper Hill, Tennessee and a graduate of Davidson College, a topnotch liberal arts institution in North Carolina.

Howell asked me what experience I had. I told him about my brief time at CBS and WTCR and how I had rubbed elbows with some famous people working as a fill-in prop guy on the Jimmy Dean Show. Howell easily saw through my "smoke" since my experience had nothing to do with the sports writing job. As the interview started slipping away I peeked his interest when I started talking about Johnny Majors, the then famous quarterback at the University of Tennessee, a subject I knew something about from talking with people in Kentucky who constantly talked in detail about their biggest nemesis on the gridiron. All of a sudden Howell and I had something in common and we discussed sports for an over an hour. Finally Howell said: "Reilly, I'm going to give you a shot. There's a football game in Seoul on Saturday. You cover it and I want the copy in as early as possible because I'm going to send it over to Stripes."   He meant Stars 'n' Stripes, a civilian run newspaper based in Toyko that circulated throughout the Far East for military personnel and civilian government workers.

Fear ran up and down my spine like I had never experienced before or since. Howell had called my bluff. But I was between, as they say, " a rock and a hard place." If I backed out of the challenge, like I wanted to do, there's was an excellent chance I'd be transferred up to the demilitarized zone that separated South and North Korea as punishment for failing in my job as a company clerk. Howell said he would send the departing sports editor to the game to help me out. That provided some relief and the challenge was accepted.

When I got to the football game the departing sports editor took off to unknown places with a Korean woman and left me to fend for myself. I had no idea what to do so I wrote down almost every play and asked some of the other sports writers what they thought of the game. My notes were a mess but I did get the final score right.

Back in the office Howell said he needed the copy within an hour. When two hours had passed he walked over to my desk, saw I hadn't written very much and said "holy cow" or something like that (I don't remember Howell ever swearing). But he was visibly upset and took the notes and asked me to describe what I saw. He turned that mess of mine into a decent story, a remarkable feat, and sent it off to Stripes.

I held my head in my hands, doing everything I could to keep from crying, and began mentally preparing myself to serve as a foot soldier. Millions of men had done it and so could I, although it would be a difficult adjustment after having served in two feather soft jobs while lacking the ability to hit the side of a barn with a rifle shot.

As he walked toward the door Howell said without looking at me "show up at 8 on Monday." I wanted to hug him but it would have been difficult placing my short skinny arms around his rather hefty physique. I did show up on Monday and Howell introduced me to Capt. Hartell, an officer with an attitude similar Mash's Colonel Henry Blake. He quickly approved my transfer to the Cavalier staff. Master Sergeants Pace and Minor, the two top copy editors, were told to give me a two-week crash course in journalism. They critiqued my copy with out mercy, tearing each sentence apart with a black pencil. At first I didn't think I'd make it. Transforming ideas and events into understandable simple sentences was completely new to me. I didn't write much in high school except for some short answers to test questions and many times the teacher found it difficult to decipher what I had written.

By the second week I got a hang of it and by the end of that week I put together a pretty good story. I eventually was given a regular column, "From the Horse's Mouth. " I also had most my stories and some of my photographs reprinted in Stars n Stripes and a few of them even appeared in the worldwide Army Times. I traveled to Tokyo on assignment twice and worked alone sleeping with the troops in the field or at one of the Recreation Centers five days a week. I was also promoted to E-4, an administrative rank equivalent to corporal.

Being promoted wasn't easy in Korea. It took me two tries to get my extra stripe. Many military occupational specialties suspended all promotions at the time. Candidates for promotion had to answer questions before a Military Board of officers and enlisted men. Preference for promotion was given to combat ready troops and justifiably so.

At that time I earned enough to save some money. I stayed away from the Whore House, didn't drink the cheap booze or smoke the cheap cigarettes and didn't take side trips to Hong Kong. My goal was to survive the tour in good health and learn something. One day Sergeant Pace, a short, balding guy who looked much older than his age, motioned for me to walk over to the tennis court where he was playing a match with another soldier. Speaking through the wire fence he said: "Reilly, you can write. But if you want to be a journalist you had better start reading more books and newspapers." He turned and walked away continuing on with his tennis game.

My tour ended abruptly. It was about ten in the morning and I was still sleeping at one of the Recreation Centers after doing a late night interview when a private from another outfit came in and tapped my shoulder. "They want you at headquarters," he said. "Follow me."

Red Cross had notified headquarters that my father Harry was seriously ill and they were sending me home. Instinctively I knew my father was dead but didn't say anything.

When the Army wants to move it can move fast as hell. The guys in the office packed my bags while I processed out of the First Calvary Division. I was driven to Kimpo Air Base in Seoul and given a top priority flight to Tokyo. I then boarded a civilian plane to San Francisco and transferred to a civilian flight headed to New York City.

The Kinny Funeral Home in Sharon, Connecticut was handling my father's burial. The Kinnys were our cousins on my father's side and had conducted funerals for the family of the late William F. Buckley, a public intellectual and founder of the National Review magazine. I was born in Sharon Hospital but lived when I was an infant in nearby Amenia, New York just across the border from Connecticut.

My father Harry was 55 years older than me and the large age difference kept us from a normal father and son relationship. We didn't hunt and fish together, or play ball in the backyard or go on vacations. He never attended my baseball or basketball games and he wasn't interested in my schooling. He liked baseball and in the 1940s we use to listen to the Brooklyn Dodger games on the radio. He enjoyed listening to Amos n Andy, Jack Benny, Fibber McGee and Molly, and the Lone Ranger. He would discuss politics with some of our relatives while playing pinochle but I never saw him read a book. He was short and over weight, rolled his own cigarettes and sat in an old chair in the basement of the apartment we rented in Poughkeepsie, his getaway from his four children and their friends.

Years later my father had a leg amputated. He used to wiz around his small apartment in a wheel chair near the end of his life. He never complained to me. According to family lore he was once a successful small businessman who owned a restaurant, motel and a couple of gas pumps near Amenia. People drove up from New York City to escape the urban heat and stopped to eat, possible stay the night and drive away with a tank of gas. My father extended credit to his regular customers and was done in by the Great Depression. My mother Elsa, who worked along side my father, said some of their customers were literally wealthy one day and paupers the next. "Some took their own lives," she said.

My father's occupation was listed as an unemployed laborer on my birth certificate several years into the depression. When World War 11 arrived he joined the ranks of people employed in the defense industry.

The thing about my father was that he was so normal for the time. He moved around a lot looking for work. He had to scratch out a living, had no pension, savings and just enough intelligence and ambition to muddle through life. His greatest gift to me was to have no great expectations, to let me grow up on my own and at my own pace.

Following my father's funeral I returned to Washington to await re-assignment. The Army wasn't going to send me back to Korea since I had less than two months left on my overseas tour of duty. I was disappointed because I had filed an inter theater transfer request to work for Star n Stripes in Tokyo. I did the next best thing and asked my brother's friend, Ted Venetoulis, if he could help out. Mr. Venetoulis, now a civilian again, was an administrative assistant for a congressman from Maryland. He made a phone call to the Pentagon and the Army assigned me to Fort Belvoir, its engineering center outside Washington. The Army reasoned it wouldn't need to pay my travel expenses following my discharge within the next year. I lucked out by landing the job as a sports editor for The Castle, Ft. Belvoir's post newspaper. The top editor was Robert Ritchie, a prominent writer and editor for The Intercollegiate Studies Institute (ISI), a politically conservative journal, and Jerry Carter, the assistant editor who would later become a professor at Saint Boneventure University. Both had master's degrees.

Mr. Carter and I went out virtually every night after work to a bar and restaurant. There were usually eight to ten of us sitting around tables pushed together. The conversations were mostly about politics. Mr. Carter and I also distributed the base newspaper driving around in his black French Peugeot while Greek opera star Maria Callas sang her heart out on tape. He would sing along for a while, stop and then describe the story. Mr. Carter not only loved Ms. Callas' voice but her ability as a dramatic actress. I met him at his home 15 years later and he still was talking about his love for Maria Callas.

They were fun days. President John F. Kennedy had assumed the presidency and there was a youthful optimism throughout the capitol. I was promoted to E-5, the equivalent to a buck sergeant, and earned an extra $30 a month by passing a proficiency test (P1) that was listed on my discharge papers. My military occupation was officially an Information Specialist, a designation I received without attending formal classes. I had been in the Army less than three years and outranked many soldiers who were older and far more educated.

Over the years I've tried to figure out some things.

How much was my on- the- job education worth in dollar terms? Was it as valuable as having attended the same college for three years, surrounded basically by the same students and professors? Was reading a book and completing written assignments a better way to learn than by actually learning the work on the job and then performing the task?

Our forefathers learned things on the job. They built their own homes, they grew their own food, they tended to the sick, they taught themselves to read and write, they taught themselves the law by reading Blackstone. They had no choice. They were on their own. Why have we down played this type of learning?

We're on our own today, facing an unknown future and the "wilderness" of the 21st century. People will have to learn things on the fly to keep up with the fast pace of society yet the emphasis is being placed on learning in schools and colleges doing what the teacher and professor say. Is this the right learning approach for a rapidly changing world? Will the people who can learn on their own have an advantage over those who can't or won't learn on their own?

My achievements were virtually nonexistent compared to some big time on the job learners. Chuck Yeager, the first pilot to break the sound barrier, Audie Murphy, the nation's most decorated soldier, Paul McCartney, the most successful song-writer-performer in pop history, Vivien Thomas, a cardiac surgery pioneer with a high school education, tErnest Hemingway, Nobel prize winner with a revolutionary writing style. The list of on the job geniuses is endless and yet modern society acts as if they never existed.

What my real life, non book early education taught me was I had a lot to learn, my faults were substantial, my talent limited, the world didn't revolve around me, and there were very smart and talented people at all levels of life, that adaptability was the key to survival and that this nation can not survive without the support and dedication of the common man and woman.

I knew at a young age I wasn't qualified to lead anyone's band. I didn't have the political skills to reach the upper level of a profession. The small achievements meant I had some worth. Yet my limitations didn't diminish me as a person although some would argue they did. What is important was that society benefited because I recognized my limitations and stepped aside by not holding a position I wasn't entitled to. I benefited because I didn't reach beyond my capacity and found joy in simple things that didn't involve lots of money or power.

But I lived an interesting life as I was given the opportunity to interview famous and influential people throughout a 35-year journalism career ranging from Nobel Prize winning scientist Willis Lamb to Globetrotter Meadowlark Lemmon, the crown prince of basketball. My on-the-job training prepared me well for that kind of work.

I'm glad I learned the hard lessons of life early on, particularly my limitations. It made life so much easier and more realistic as I grew older. That's why I support on- the -job training.

(3)
Health Care: It Makes Me Sick

Americans spend an estimated $2.7 trillion dollars a year on health care while history shows most people could, if they wanted to, take care of a number of their own aches and pains and avoid the cost of doctors, nurses and drugs.

We have been led to believe that modern medicine is necessary to blunt any pain while enabling us to live longer lives than our ancestors.

I did a little historical research and found that people in the 1700 and 1800s, when there was no sanitation or modern conveniences like inside toilets, often took good care of themselves and other members of their family.

Abigail Adams (1744-1818), one of the most fascinating women in American history, was so sick in her youth she couldn't attend school. Yet she lived to age 74 and took care of her own health, the health of her husband John and their five children (a sixth was stillborn). She also cared for her sister and mother.

That was just one of her tasks. Mrs. Adams lived on a farm for many years and tutored her children, took care of the livestock, cooked, cleaned, made some her own cloths, and helped out members of the Continental Army when they would stop by at all hours of the day and night. She was an intellectual and an advocate of women's rights so elegantly expressed in one of her many letters to her husband:

"I long to hear that you have declared an independency. And, by the way, in the new code of laws which I suppose it will be necessary for you to make, I desire you would remember the ladies and be more generous and favorable to them than your ancestors." And then she included a nice little touch. "Do not put such unlimited power into the hands of the husbands. All men would be tyrants if they could."

To get an idea of how long people lived in the 1700 and 1800s I used as a sample the 32 men considered the Founders of our country. Eight of the Founders reached their eighties, eight reached their seventies, eleven lived to their sixties, three made it into their fifties and two died in their forties.

Quite remarkable considering everyday was a fight for survival in a terrible environment with wild animals and diseases galore. If anyone believes modern medicine has somehow made us hardier and healthier than our forefathers than I suggest they consider my argument based on the 1983 comedy "Trading Places," starring Eddie Murphy and Dan Aykroyd. Instead of con artist Murphy switching places with blue blood Aykroyd to prove born or made under Social Darwinism's survival of the fittest tenet, one Founder and Abigail Adams will, by my hand, mythically switch places with a Wall Street Master of the Universe and his wife.

How would a Wall Street trophy wife fare getting out of bed at sunrise in the 1800s to gather food, prepare breakfast, work in the garden, spin wool, tutor the children, tend to a sick parent in a house that has no running water, no electricity, no refrigerator and no insulation and is basically a fire trap? How would she fair on a month long boat trip from Boston to London to Paris with a bunch of smelly passengers?

How would her $50 million bonus baby husband fare riding a worn out horse down a muddy road to the local tavern to do business with men who hadn't bathed in a month gathered together in a room with drunks, strangers, horse thieves, and tough guys who'd knock his block off if he looked at them? How would he react to eating food that may or may not have been cooked right on a plate where roaches may have been before he was?

How long would this gilded-age society twosome, brought up on modern medicine, fine food and servants, last on the frontier?

Let's resurrect and fast- forward Abigail Adams to 2009. How would Abigail fare if she could sleep to noon, have her meal in bed and cloths laid out perfectly to slip on? Then a message and hair makeover at the local salon before the mid-afternoon trip to Sacs Fifth Avenue to purchase a $6,000 evening dress, then on for a couple of drinks with the ladies, a nap and finally a night at the opera. The following morning she would fly off to Paris in a private luxury jet plane to avoid congested airports, uncomfortable seats and inconvenient flight schedules.

And how would one of Founders adjust if he were picked up at his $20 million Fifth Ave. New York City apartment by a chauffeur and then driven by limousine to the airport where he boarded a private jet for a flight to a magnificent high- rise office building where two gentlemen greeted him in an office with $10 million worth of furnishings, including a $35,000 wooden umbrella rack?

Who statistically would live the longest in their new environment, the Master of the Universe couple or Abigail Adams and one of the Founders?

If we asked registered voters to decide what couple helped our country the most who would they select?

The " Changing Places" is a simple metaphor for what America was and what it has become.

Many of our ancestors were obviously physically superior to millions of Americans today who rush to the doctor when they get a little pain and can't walk four blocks to Starbucks without running out of breath. Modern day athletes, although they achieve agility and speed, often flame out by age fifty like a roman candle.

The typical female born today is expected to live to age 83 and the male to age 78, according to recent federal government statistics, in the same age range of tens of thousands of men and women who lived in the 1700 and 1800s. Our forefathers died from incidents having nothing to do with medical care such as being mauled by a bear, being killed from falling off a horse, dying from exposure to extreme weather. They also died in droves from hunger. As did over seven million people during the Great Depression of the 1930s, according to a study titled "The American Famine," by researcher Boris Borisov.

When I was growing up in the 1940s and 1950s most people had a knack for knowing when to see a doctor. And they didn't have the vast amount of information that's now available on the Internet.

The trouble with medicine is there are no guarantees. Modern medicine can do some marvelous things but it can also screw up. Two former colleagues died from complications following surgery and one from an improperly diagnosed heart condition.

The advantages today in medicine are in such areas as advanced surgical procedures, diagnoses, making patients more comfortable, relieving pain and suffering while reducing response time to medical emergencies. Still it's estimated 150,000 patients nationwide unnecessarily die each year from preventable mishaps in hospitals and that we have a higher infant mortality rate than many other industrialized nations. Too often the operation proved a success but the patient died during recovery.

Physical health, like a true education, rests a lot with how an individual approaches personal issues and not with doctors. Having insurance and modern medicine available doesn't necessarily mean a person will be healthier. Some times the person with medical coverage takes more chances knowing a hospital bed will be waiting if the drugs he takes are too powerful or the drinks he downs are too strong.

Millions of Americans are slowly and deliberately killing themselves with drugs thereby offsetting some of the advances of modern medicine. According to federal government statistics listed on the Internet an estimated 371 billion cigarettes were consumed in the United States in 2006 at a cost of $82 billion even though nearly every youngster and adult knows cigarettes kill.

One hundred billion dollars was spent on alcohol and even more money to fight alcohol abuse.

An estimated 2.8 million Americans are chronic cocaine users, and about 900,000 were chronic heroine users.

About 3,2 million people are occasional users of cocaine and 250,000 occasional users of heroine. Nearly 600,000 people use methamphetamines.

Nine years ago Americans spent about $36 billion on cocaine, $10 billion on heroine, $5.4 billion on methamphetamines, eleven billion on marijuana and $2.4 billion on other illegal drugs. In New York City alone it's estimated that more than $800 million a year is spent on illegal drugs.

Illegal drugs are flowing into United States at such an astounding rate that we are conducting military type of operations to stop it. With that amount of drugs entering the country to be willingly consumed by millions of people there is not much modern medicine can do to help.

Why must the public pick up the medical bills of those who willingly destroy their bodies? The nation can't afford it. People who use illegal drugs should suffer the consequences including paying for their own medical care. No government or corporate paid insurance coverage for them. Hospitals should not only have the right but the obligation to refuse treatment to illegal drug users who can't pay the bill.

If the government sends young men and women overseas to die in the fight against terrorism then the government should automatically execute convicted drug dealers as enemy combatants in the war against illegal drugs. Drug dealers are as violent and a threat to the country as any terrorist.

Then there are the legal drugs that millions of people are taking daily that can cause side effects such as stroke, internal bleeding, heart attacks, bladder failure and death.

Potential lethal legal drugs are advertised 24/7 on television and radio stations, beginning in the era of deregulation of the 1980s. I can't figure out the difference of being killed by a legal drug I took to reduce my blood pressure or a heavy dose of the illegal cocaine I took to get a high. I'm dead. I'm history. I wouldn't think much of anyone who tried to convince me to take a pill that could possibly kill. Uncle Sam doesn't care. He allows potentially killer drugs to be advertised on television like shirts and shoes.

The medical profession is profit driven therefore the financial incentive is having plenty of sick people to treat therefore the emphasis is placed on promoting drugs and insurance (guaranteeing the health provider is paid) rather than publicizing proven home remedies and wellness. If sickness results in huge corporate profits how can we ever expect the government to support a physically and mentally healthy nation based on proven home remedies that don't cost much?

Then there is the social problem connected with advertising legal drugs. A few popular drugs with serious side effects are being advertised on prime time television touting the joys of the four-hour erection. A lot of boys and girls four and five years old are sitting in front of the television screen listening and watching the erection advertisements year after year. I don't claim to be the late Dr. Benjamin Spock yet advertisements about erections don't seem appropriate for kids headed toward puberty. It could be a little dicey by the time they reach junior high. All the drug makers had to do to promote their product was send an e-mail to members of the over the hill gang looking to spice up their sex life.

Advertising legal drugs should be banned from the airways

All this stuff about drugs and self- destructive behavior is bad enough and then the federal government has to constantly remind us that the cost of medical care is bankrupting the country and it needs to be reformed. It's giving us nightmares. Yet the health care problem and costs have gotten worse over the years. All talk, no meaningful reform. Uncle Sam loves to keep us on edge.

To make matters worse we constantly hear about every possible ailment under the sun. It's enough to scare us. A little pimple grows and people think they have cancer. They cough and think it's a serious lung problem. They get tired at work and buy a pill to jack them selves up. The media and the government would do more good promoting up to date drug- free home remedies and personal responsibility. How about more stories on people who have been successful managing their health without medicines or visits to the doctor? Doris Eaton Travis, the last surviving Ziegfeld girl, briefly made the news lately when at age 105 she returned to the stage she left nearly a century ago and kicked up her heels a bit. She avoids most medical care therefore should be the poster woman of good health with her picture and story spread across the United States. People can and do live happily without popping pills!

And, like education, we should be able get home remedies on the cheap. We should be able to take home health care to another level.   .

We need professional health care but it shouldn't be profit driven. Yet Washington won't help us there. Individuals and their families must take charge of their health by not abusing their bodies and avoiding doctors except when they think its necessary. Only then will the nation's medical bills drop like a rock.

And people must learn to see through the medical propaganda.

A few years ago it was commonly believed every man over age fifty should be tested for prostrate cancer. There was money to be made by testing prostates. Now the effectiveness of the prostrate test is being questioned. Someone caught the honesty shakes.

What has modern medicine has done for our youth? Millions of kids are slow, fat and diabetic. Schools have dropped physical education programs. Most of the kids would be better off with an ax to chop wood rather than a pill to pop or medicine to swallow. Trim the kids down with exercise. Keep them away from the fast foods and sweets. Keep them away from the drugs sold near the school door. That's less expensive than a visit to the doctor.

What needs to be done to reduce medical costs? First, the government shouldn't do business with medical firms who are listed on the stock exchanges or who pay dividends.

Big money shouldn't be made at the expense of the sick.

Two, It needs to tear down the entire Medicare system and rebuild it to eliminate waste, corruption, and over billing. It must also make some difficult choices of end of life medical services. Spending tens of thousands of dollars to extend a life that for all intense and purpose has ended except for the last breath, is not the government's responsibility. Death is a part of living and if it comes sooner than later so be it. If someone wants to extend life as long as possible then he or she should pay for a private insurance policy.

Medicare should only be available for people age 70 and over. No exceptions. Separate programs should be adopted to meet the needs of people under age 70, particularly young people who generally don't have as many health problems as the elderly.

The public must also be held responsible. If a person decides to smoke, take drugs and engage in other destructive behavior then the government shouldn't bear any of the financial costs of their medical care. Medicine should only be a human right for people who do the best they can to take care of their health. Why should the public care about a person's health if they don't care about it themselves? We always hear about people's rights. But we never hear about a person's responsibility to society. That should change. Destructive behavior shouldn't be rewarded. People who want to light up should pay up and purchase their own health coverage. And that should apply to the elderly as well.

The government could drastically reduce medical costs if it had the will do so. Right now the government is clinging to its old ways of letting market driven companies dictate policy that includes making many people rich. Medicine shouldn't be a Wall Street cash cow yet that's exactly what it's become. A few years ago my wife had a heart attack. The one-half block ambulance ride cost $650, $200 more than a round trip ticket for two from Phoenix to New York City at the time. Padding medical bills costs the nation tens of billions of dollars annually. If the government would get down to the real business of cleaning up the mess instead of complaining about the cost we wouldn't be a nation holding a tin cup in its hand.

On a somewhat brighter note miracles do happen. Even in Washington. Let's say for argument sake Congress does pass a medical reform bill that includes universal health insurance coverage.

If that happens there will be a big celebration in Washington. A lot of big names will gathered on the White House lawn. Self- congratulatory speeches will be delivered and maybe even the Marine Corp. Band will show up.

However, according to the proposals I've read if a bill guaranteeing health coverage for everyone is signed into law it's not going to stop one person from taking drugs. It's not going to stop people from smoking and excessive drinking. It's not going to get the overweight dude off the coach and out of the house for a two- mile walk. It's not going to make the nation healthier. And it won't reduce medical costs like it should.

But I do know what the bill will do. It will line a lot of pockets.

(4)
A Rule That Is Ruining The Law Profession

To understand why it costs so much to hire a lawyer the public must first understand how the law profession controls legal education that helps jack up the price people pay for their day in court. The last thing the legal profession wants is a load of invisible money. Reducing legal costs doesn't appear to be high on the profession's agenda.

A complex law case can cost $200,000 or more. Many attorneys charge fees of $150 to $250 an hour at a time when the typical American earns $16 an hour.

If legal education didn't cost so much more people would have a chance to earn a law license including single parents, retirees, career switchers and those who wish to serve society. And these non- traditional lawyers could bring down costs of legal services while adding more maturity and real life experience among the ranks of practitioners.

I started thinking about the high cost of a legal education in 1977 when a young married couple from California came into the newsroom at The Arizona Republic, the morning newspaper in Phoenix where I was working as a reporter.

The couple was upset. They had both graduated from the Western States College of Law in San Diego and had passed the California Bar Exam, a three- day test that's one of the most demanding bar exams in the nation. They both had successfully practiced law and had good recommendations. But they could not take the Arizona Bar Exam although Western States College of Law had the same curriculum as the majority of law schools in the nation and had received approval from the California Committee of Bar Examiners, an accrediting agency.

Here's the rub. Western States had not received recognition from the Chicago based American Bar Association (ABA), the only accrediting agency sanctioned by the U.S. Department of Education and therefore the Arizona Supreme Court wouldn't let the couple take its bar exam. Arizona only recognizes ABA approved law schools. California, however, is one of the few states that permits graduates of non-ABA approved law schools to take its bar exam.

In other words, California allows students to earn a law license for far less money if they chose to do so because students have several ways to earn a law license including apprenticeships. Forty- seven other states, including Arizona, forces law students to pay a higher price for a legal education because ABA approval is extremely expensive for a law college because of its mandates involving the number of full time faculty allowed compared to part-time faculty and the size of the law library. Non- ABA law schools have more flexibility in keeping operating costs down.

The legal profession likes to claim law schools matter. They do but not as much as we are led to believe. In China some students learned the law in a cave. Abe Lincoln learned a lot of law by reading books under an apple tree and he represented some major corporate clients. Robert Jackson, the United States chief prosecutor at the Nuremberg Trials following World War 11, was the last Supreme Court Justice not to have graduated law school. President Harry S. Truman seriously thought of nominating Jackson to be chief justice. No Supreme Court Justice in American history has matched the brilliance of John Marshall and he had about three years of formal schooling. Marshall's and Jackson's record on the court suggest people today could be elevated to the high court from apprenticeship and other programs yet we are led to believe only graduates of elite law schools qualify (eight of the nine justices earned their law degree from an Ivy League school).

There is no legitimate reason for that. Bill Gates and Steve Jobs, two non- college graduates, founded Microsoft and Apple, two of the most important high tech companies in the world. It's far more difficult finding people to fill the top echelon jobs at Microsoft and Apple than it is to find people to fill seats on the U.S. Supreme Court. In other words, it takes more mental power to land a rover on Mars than to read or write a legal opinion but we wouldn't know it by the small applicant pool of potential justices a president considers when the vacancy occurs on the court. Appointing a social scientist to the court, perhaps a political science expert from outside the legal and east establishments, wouldn't be a bad idea. The nominee would have a different perspective and no judicial record for dissenters to pick a part to advance narrow political causes. It would be worth a try.

While a lot of the legal profession remained mired in old traditions, the cost of a legal education kept rising through the years. I wrote about the bar rule issue again in the early 1990s prompted by scholarly reports stating the country needed to adopt more apprenticeship programs in such areas a law, medicine, engineering and journalism. Apprenticeship programs would add diversity and a fresh of breath air to the well-worn academic path most people take to obtain a professional skill.

The Arizona Supreme Court wasn't interested. It failed to properly examine the merit of its bar exam ruling. It failed to take expert testimony from specialists in learning theory and higher education in general that would have shed light on the issue. The court never contacted the California Committee of Bar Examiners to see how the graduates of non- ABA law schools performed compared to graduates of ABA law schools. The court never contacted the State of Washington's Bar Association to find out how well the graduates of apprenticeship law programs did inside and outside the courtroom. It never bothered to interview any of the non- traditional law students in California or the State of Washington to see how they measured up in person. The bar rule decision was a decision made without substantial research and serious thought.

. The bar rule is a throwback to the discriminatory practices of the 19th and early part of the 20th century when the elite members of the legal profession didn't want blacks and women to practice law. Those days of discrimination against blacks and women are long gone but the bar exam rule remains in place to restrain competition as much as possible to keep prices high in both legal education and legal practice. What else could it be?

I've been in Arizona 36 years and have never heard the bar exam rule justified in detail by either a member of the bar association or the Supreme Court. There are about one million lawyers in the U.S. so it should be easy for the legal profession to find a member to write a brief justifying the rule.

The public should also know more about the history of the ABA because it directly affects the life of everyone living in this country.

The history of the ABA was brilliantly discussed by Jerold Auerbach, a Professor of History at Wellesley College, in his 1976 book "Unequal Justice: Lawyers and Social Change in Modern America."

Here is what Harvard Law Professor Alan Dershowitz, writing in the New York Times Book Review, said about Auerbach's book:

"In this remarkable book about America's elite lawyers and their quest for power and profit, Jerold S. Auerbach goes a long way toward explaining why lawyers have played such central roles in perpetuating so many injustices, ranging from racial and religious discrimination, to McCarthyism, to the denial of legal representation to the poor…Unequal Justice stands as a powerful and well documented indictment of the elite bar's failure to live up to the trust that has been bestowed upon it by our system of justice."

Milton S. Gould, writing in the New York Law Journal, wrote: "He (Auerbach) cuts through the cant and hypocrisy with which our profession too often defends itself from lay criticism. The infamous, ethnic, religious, social and economic snobbery which disgraced our profession for a hundred years are exposed and analyzed with surgical skills, and the effects of these dark forces on the legal community…"

"This book should be read and seriously considered by all lawyers who are interested in the future of the legal profession in America…(Unequal Justice) shakes the foundations in a particularly way. We should be disturbed…I can only urge you to read this book and search your own soul." John E. Cribbet, American Bar Association Journal.

Auerbach's book should be required reading in high school so students would begin to appreciate the impact law has on society and why they should pay attention to what goes on in the legal profession.

Now it's time to address another central issue involving the bar exam rule. Does accreditation do what people are led to believe it does? The answer is no.

George Leef, a member of the National Association of Scholars, summed up what literally hundreds of neutral observers concluded: "Accreditation—of law schools as well as undergraduate institutions—is no guarantee of good academic quality. When the ABA or other accrediting associations evaluate a school, the focus is scarcely on the nature of the instruction at all. Rather, the key to getting and staying accredited is overwhelming a matter of inputs and procedures. When the ABA passes judgment on a law school, it looks at such matters as the size of the library, the teaching load of the faculty, and (of course) the extent of which the school is 'diverse.' Whether the classes are taught competently is not directly investigated, but they are presumed to be as long as the school's inputs and procedures look right."

Mr. Leef's article was published on March 16, 2006 by The John Pope Center for Higher Education Policy.

College presidents, professors, economists, and some government officials for years complained about the accrediting system. Articles have been published in numerous publications including "The Chronicle of Higher Education."

Some academics counter Leef's arguments saying accreditation is voluntary. That's true. But graduates of unaccredited programs can't transfer their credits to accredited schools, can't qualify for many loans and grants, are prohibited from being considered for admission to the vast majority of graduate programs and have a difficult time getting a good job.

The voluntary argument attached to accreditation is simply a ruse wrapped around a fiction.

A few states are progressive and honest about the legitimate ways to learn the law. The fact is many graduates of apprenticeship programs are better lawyers than graduates of traditional law schools. They often have more professional experience –such as a doctor who earns a law degree and specializes medical cases. Some traditional law schools don't even teach the nuts and bolts of practicing law in an effort to avoid being labeled a trade school. All non-ABA law schools emphasize the actual practice of law.

It would seem the legal profession would serve society better if it concentrated on making sure its members met high standards of practice and obeyed the Rules of Professional Conduct rather than worrying about how someone actually learned the law. The bar exams could be up graded to include a skills test such as requiring applicants to demonstrate an ability to argue a case in court. Some young attorneys hang their shingle as soon as they receive certification and this worries many veteran litigators, some of whom serve as volunteer mentors to reduce the number of unsupervised greenhorns practicing law.

Any change in the bar rule must start with the U.S. Department of Education that recognizes the ABA as the sole accreditation body for the legal profession. With the backing of Uncle Sam, the privately run ABA does pretty much what it wants including adding hundreds of millions of dollars a year to the cost of law school.

If the federal government wanted to get the most "bang for the buck" in legal education it would decertify the ABA. It would demand that all the states permit qualified applicants to sit for the bar exam or all federal money would be cut off. Why should the federal government support a private organization that denies qualified people the right to take an exam to earn a living? Isn't this a prime example of the federal government supporting the interest of a private group over the interests of the general public?

The elite members of the bar association have not served the public well. The regulations needed to keep business and government in check proved inadequate as the nation heads toward bankruptcy. Lawyers write regulations. It's the lawyers who find legal loopholes to get around the restraints needed to keep institutions in check. We need a large and new cadre of lawyers trained outside of the traditional law schools with the ability and authority to challenge the elite lawyers on critical issues on behalf of the common man and woman. This won't happen so long as the federal government serves as the water boy for the American Bar Association. The public needs to pressure the Congress with letters and phone calls. The time to act is now.

(5)
Looking For Mayberry

Higher education is going broke as state legislators are forced to cut back millions of dollars in funding. College students are going broke by borrowing money to earn a credential that may or may not result in a decent paying job or any job at all.

The medical profession is broke yet there is a move to qualify 48 million more people for medical insurance although no one knows for sure if there are enough doctors and nurses to serve the nation's medical needs let alone pick up the added costs of the insurance.

The legal profession is in disarray as communities struggle financially to keep the justice system from collapsing. The men's prison in Chino, California is operating at twice its capacity. The same conditions exist at other California prisons. There is a possibility many prisoners may be released early because there isn't enough room in the big house where 174,000 bad guys live in facilities designed for 100,000 inmates. In Oregon the courts are closed on Friday's at least until 2010.

"Landlords trying to evict tenants, tenants trying to protest poor living conditions, businesses trying to collect unpaid debts, drivers fighting speeding tickets, couples going through divorces and single parents seeking child support will be among the many who will be affected," according to the Oregonian, the daily newspaper in Portland.

"The delays also could make it difficult for courts to meet the constitutional guarantee of a speedy trial. Some defendants may have to be released pending trial or, in a worse case scenario, judges may be forced to dismiss charges," the newspaper wrote.

There have been reports that some prosecutors aren't pursuing criminal cases because they lack the manpower and money to do so.

When money is short some hard choices must be made. What's more important cutting funds for higher education when there are tested ways to get a higher education on the cheap or to cut vital public services such as fire and police when there are not clear cut cost saving alternatives?

Many states are reducing essential services rather than raise taxes. But are the priorities right? Is it worth funding failing schools (students can learn outside the classroom) at the expense of trash pickup, health clinics, safe roads, food banks and employment services?

On the federal level the government just keeps borrowing money at a level not seen in human history. What efforts have been made to save money other than efforts to cut back on programs for the public such as the school lunch program and services for wounded veterans?

Members of Congress seldom mention the need to redesigned federal agencies to conform to the realities of the 21st century. It hasn't done enough to eliminate corruption in federal programs such as defense and medical care, it hasn't called on the American people to make sacrifices for the national good (such as national service) and it hasn't done enough to get rid of the drug trade that's threatening the very fiber of American life.

And the federal government doesn't tell the truth to the American people. A few weeks before the financial collapse we were told the nation's economy was "basically sound, " a deception similar to Iraq having weapons of mass destruction that were supposedly poised and ready to blow us up. Every time the stock market goes up, every time the unemployment rate goes down, or there is an up tick in consumer confidence the government gives the impression things are getting better. But they are not getting better. The most serious problems facing this nation can't be solved for years.

If reform is to come it will have to come from the common man and woman. Governments are too beholden to special interest s to voluntarily bring about needed reforms. That's not hard to understand. Most of the leaders in Congress are re-elected. Most of the high-level government jobs are given to people politically connected and who in private life often worked for the companies that caused the problems in the first place.

It may take 15 to 20 years before we understand the impact today's government policies had on the nation. It may take that long to know if we should have move quicker to develop virtual universities, slowed down the growth in students loans, emphasized home health remedies and made the legal profession more accountable to the public. The criticism of a public policy shouldn't be placed in the context of today but in the context of two decades from now. And that isn't easy for anyone to do.

Some people are attempting to reduce the stress of modern living by changing their lifestyle.

Remember Mayberry? Andy. Barney. Aunt Bee. Opie. A town where the physician makes house calls, where the attorney takes routine cases regardless of the client's the ability to pay, where people learn for the joy of learning.

While many people look for a simpler way of life others are preparing their children to reach the top of the financial ladder. They live in large cities. They prep their children to get into the finest elementary and high school. Pay thousands of dollars to prepare them to sit for standardized tests while plotting a strategy for their children to gain entrance into the nation's most elite colleges and universities. The current situation hasn't changed their idea of the good life or altered the path to get there.

In the middle there are people searching for an affluent lifestyle with upward mobility with some time left over to spend with family and friends.

Should we encourage our children to strive to be a Gordon Gekko, the fictional corporate raider in the movie "Wall Street?" Should we strive to be the fictional Andy Taylor or an Aunt Bee from Mayberry who live in the same house forever, who identify with their friends and neighbors and where ice cream and pie on Andy's porch is considered a big night out. Or is the ideal lifestyle that of Ward and June Cleaver from "Leave It To Beaver" fame who are middle class moving up in the world with a membership at the local golf club and a savings account for Wally and Theodore's college education?

Have we reached a point where some areas of science and technology are doing more harm than good for society, destroying our humanity by slowly replacing man with artificial intelligence and robots? Or should we keep traveling the current path unrestrained?

Should we have a Bill of Responsibilities to go along with our Bill of Rights? Have we placed too much emphasis on our rights and not enough on our responsibilities as citizens?

Should the nation become thrifty and create mountains of "invisible" money, or should it continue printing money?

If I receive enough replies I will publish them in a book and place it on the Internet.

Robert A. Reilly

My address is Robert Reilly, P.O. Box 309, Phoenix, Arizona 85001

The editorial content and opinions expressed in this book are the sole responsibility of Robert Reilly.